BUMPING DOTS

The Art of Serendipitous Encounters

DR. HERB THOMAS

BUMPING DOTS

The Art of Serendipitous Encounters

Herbert H. Thomas, Jr., PhD

ISBN-13: 978-1-963820-00-3 print edition
ISBN-13: 978-1-963820-01-0 e-book edition

RES
PUBLISHING & BRANDING

www.RESPublishingandBranding.com
contact@respublishingandbranding.com

DEDICATION

This book is dedicated to all dreamers and connectors—

To the curious souls who look out into the world and see not strangers but friends yet to be made. To those who understand that a single moment, a single encounter, can alter the entire course of one's life if we allow it.

Within these pages lies a legacy - the story of Bumping Dots, of serendipitous encounters, and of the threads that weave us all together. It is a narrative that has lived in the hearts of many before us and one that shall be passed on to those yet to come.

I give this book to you in hopes that it may inspire you to bump dots in your own life. To have the courage to reach out across the void and touch someone. To understand that we are not alone in this world. May you experience firsthand the power and wonder of Bumping Dots.

With joy and gratitude,
Dr. Herb

ACKNOWLEDGEMENTS

In the journey of bringing *Bumping Dots: The Art of Serendipitous Encounters* to life, the support and inspiration I have been fortunate enough to receive have been both profound and uplifting. At the very heart of this endeavor, I am deeply indebted to my beloved parents, Herbert H. Thomas Sr. and Algenia S. Thomas. Their enduring legacy of kindness, their respect for all walks of life, and their unwavering belief in the power of connection have been my compass. They taught me to see the world not just as it is but also as it could be when we reach out and truly engage with one another.

To my wife, Dr. Christine C. Thomas, your love is the cornerstone of every achievement. Your intellectual rigor and emotional support have been instrumental in shaping this work. To my children, Dr. Ashley C. Thomas and Kimberly "Duchess" Thomas, your vibrant spirits and insightful observations have enriched these pages more than words can express. Together, we sacrificed time for this project, engaged in lively discussions, and sifted through a lifetime of stories. Our time spent together as a family during this process has been the greatest gift.

I extend my heartfelt thanks to my colleagues and mentors, whose wisdom has been a guiding light, and to my friends, the "dots" who sparked our shared experiences that led to the insights within these covers. To the countless strangers who have crossed my path, often becoming friends and teachers, your stories and perspectives have been the threads that weave through the very essence of this book's message.

May this acknowledgment serve not only as a testament to those who have shaped its pages but also as an inspiration to its readers. Let it be a reminder that every person we meet has the potential to change our lives for the better, that every "bump" can lead to new horizons, and that within humanity, we each have the opportunity to be both a "dot" and a connector.

To all who hold this book in your hands, may you find within it the encouragement to embrace serendipity, to trust your intuition, and to engage deeply with the world around you. For in the art of bumping dots, we find the essence of our shared humanity and the path to a more connected and compassionate world.

With sincere gratitude,
Dr. Herb

FOREWORD

In my journey as an author, I've explored themes of perseverance, mentorship, and the unexpected twists in our paths, as seen in *Three Feet from Gold* and similar works. It is with great enthusiasm that I introduce *Bumping Dots*, a book by Dr. Herbert H. Thomas Jr. that resonates deeply with these themes.

Dr. Thomas's insightful work is a tribute to the serendipitous encounters that shape our lives, reminding us that every chance meeting holds the potential to alter our course significantly. This book delves deeper into the concept, illustrating how these unplanned interactions can lead to life-changing opportunities and insights. Through a series of compelling stories and reflections, *Bumping Dots* invites readers to look at their own lives and recognize the impact of each encounter, no matter how small or brief.

In this book, he guides us through a landscape rich with potential and possibility, encouraging us to remain open and receptive to the world around us. His narrative is not just about the power of connecting with others; it's also a deeper exploration of how these connections can lead to personal growth, professional development, and an enriched understanding of the world.

As you turn each page, you'll be inspired to view your interactions through a new lens, seeing the extraordinary possibilities hidden within everyday moments. *Bumping Dots* challenges you to embrace the serendipity in your own life, to learn from every person you meet, and to find the extraordinary in the ordinary.

I commend Dr. Thomas for creating a work that not only entertains but also educates and inspires. As you embark on this journey with *Bumping Dots*, may you find renewed appreciation for the unexpected encounters that dot your life, each one holding the promise of new horizons and unexplored paths.

Enjoy the journey and the countless discoveries that await,
Dr. Greg S. Reid

CONTENTS

INTRODUCTION

My Evolutionary Journey Coining "Bumping Dots"

As a youth, sitting in the warm embrace of my hometown church, I often marveled at the sea of faces around me – all distinct, all connected. It was in this sacred haven, amidst hymns and hope, that my journey began— a journey of understanding connection and encounters that would later be recognized as "Bumping Dots."

Bumping Dots is not simply words on a page. It isn't an academic theory coined in isolation from reality. Bumping Dots is a concept that encourages us to see each encounter with others as a chance to create meaningful connections, even in the briefest of moments. By being open, curious, and receptive to these moments, we can unlock hidden possibilities and enrich our lives through the connections we make. In other words, it's a radical transformation in the way we perceive human interaction and form bonds.

As I transitioned into my college years, I immersed myself into the excitement of athletic events and campus gatherings. I was fortunate to become the head student equipment manager for the university's football team. This role wasn't just about managing day-to-day operations such as washing uniforms, ordering equipment, ensuring practice and game-day apparatuses were in their proper place, or overseeing a staff of student equipment managers. It was also about creating a rich network of connections. Hence, I became profoundly aware of the importance of building relationships and connecting people.

You see, in my myriad of interactions and those numerous moments where my path seemed to cross or "bump" with another, there was a rhythm and an underlying pattern. It was as if every person was a dot waiting to collide with another, creating a beautiful web of intertwined destinies.

Over the years, my skill set evolved. From a keen observer in the church pews to an active participant in college life, I honed my ability to engage and connect with people from diverse backgrounds.

Yet, as life's chapters unfolded, a recurring question continued to echo in the corridors of my interactions with others. "How did you do it?" they'd ask. "How did you seize that moment?" "How did you nurture that connection?" In my younger days, I'd often attribute it to God's gifting, believing I was simply blessed in the art of communication and being a connector. But as the years progressed and my reflections deepened, I realized there was more to this "gift." It was a fusion of my personality, my unwavering desire to genuinely connect, and a recognition of the sheer power of interactions. Still, the pressing question remained: How could I translate this personal experience into a universal concept? How could I assist those who felt adrift in the vast sea of human interactions or those who yearned to build bridges and connect but didn't know how to begin?

During this reflective period, destiny introduced me to Dr. Greg S. Reid. The old adage that one person can change the trajectory of your life holds true. Greg is the Founder of Secret Knock (#1 networking business event in the world), best-selling author, filmmaker, and CEO of several businesses. He was the keynote speaker at a conference I was attending. His energetic presentation was infectious, and the information he shared was life-altering. After his presentation, I made it my mission to introduce myself to him. As I made my way through the crowd, I noticed that Greg was surrounded by many attendees. In the midst of his discourse with others, he quickly turned around, saw me, and said, "Come here and give me your phone." He took a selfie with me and began asking me questions, showing genuine interest in my ambitions and aspirations. After a conversation that lasted roughly five minutes, Greg gave me his mobile number and asked me to forward him the selfie. I did and asked him to save my number, which he did. He encouraged me to stay in touch.

Over the next few weeks, our conversations felt like masterclasses in human connection. His perspectives were the perfect complement to my experiences, bringing depth and a broader understanding of the forces at play in seemingly random encounters. Knowing Greg's busy schedule, I mustered the courage to ask if he'd mentor me. He agreed! Now I have access to Secret Knock and serve on its council. This connection has given me the opportunity to "bump dots" with CEOs, award-winning actors, best-selling authors, inventors, professional athletes, and many more.

Connecting with Greg Reid was a catalyst for me putting what was an idea into a replicable practice. I was on an expedition – a quest to decode the power behind serendipitous connections. Through intense conversations with Dr. Reid, research, introspection, and passion, the concept of Bumping Dots was birthed.

Perhaps you've felt like an observer, watching others effortlessly form connections and wondering about the secret behind their success. Or maybe you believe you're adept at forging connections but yearn to develop this skill. Regardless, Bumping Dots is an invitation to higher levels of connectivity.

You are about to embark on an experience that will unsettle, stir, and prompt you to reflect. It will compel you to consider those brief exchanges and "almost missed" opportunities to connect with others in a new light.

Bumping Dots encourages you to remain open, receptive, and ever curious, recognizing opportunities in every moment. As we delve deeper, I urge you to embrace vulnerability and let the transformative power of Bumping Dots envelop you. Challenge yourself to recognize the vast array of possibilities with every person, or "dot," you encounter.

In the realm of Bumping Dots, we discover that every chance encounter is a canvas for potential, every conversation a bridge to new horizons, and every shared moment a step towards the symphony of serendipity that connects us all.

CHAPTER ONE
What is Bumping Dots?

Bumping Dots

[bəmp iNG däts] **noun.**

A concept that recognizes how encounters ("bumps") between individuals ("dots") have the potential to form connections and reveal the beauty of serendipitous interactions.

bumping dots

[bəmp iNG däts] **verb.**

to be fully present during encounters ("bumps") with other individuals ("dots") as a way of cultivating serendipitous connections.

Bumping Dots is a concept that recognizes how encounters ("bumps") between individuals ("dots") have the potential to form connections and reveal the beauty of serendipitous interactions. These interactions can happen in various contexts, such as running into an old friend in an unexpected place, striking up a conversation with a stranger who becomes an important contact, or encountering an opportunity that one was not actively seeking. The essence of serendipity in these interactions is that they are happy accidents—unexpected yet resulting in a positive experience or outcome.

The experience of bumping dots is far from passive. It is the practice of being fully present when encountering someone, navigating beyond superficial interactions, and choosing to actively listen, communicate effectively, and showcase vulnerability. It's a dynamic and evolving exchange that invigorates both the heart and mind. As you delve into the world of Bumping Dots, you embark on a transformative expedition of growth, exploration, and continuous learning, recognizing the profound impact of each serendipitous encounter.

Through the pages of *Bumping Dots*, you're invited to explore and appreciate the world with a fresh perspective, recognizing the potential in every moment for a special and valuable meeting. Embrace the expedition and let *Bumping Dots* illuminate your path with the light of meaningful connections and boundless opportunities.

What Bumping Dots is Not

Bumping dots is distinctly different from networking. Networking, while valuable, often carries a professional, outcome-based, or utilitarian focus, aimed at expanding professional contacts, opportunities, and resources. It operates on a level of professional development and mutual benefit in the career or business domain. Networking involves strategic interactions with the objective of professional advancement.

Unlike the calculated approach of networking, bumping dots is about embracing the spontaneity of life, understanding that every person we encounter carries the potential to form connections. It's about recognizing the value in every interaction, seeing beyond the surface to the intricate web of possibilities that lie within each encounter. When bumping dots, there is an acknowledgement that connections don't only occur in professional settings or pre-planned events. They also happen during ordinary and mundane moments of life, such as in the smiles exchanged with a stranger, in the casual conversation struck up while waiting in line, or in the shared laughter with a neighbor. It's about being open, receptive, and present, understanding that every space and place is a field ripe with the potential for meaningful connections.

Benefits of Bumping Dots

In the exploration of unexpected connections, numerous advantages quickly become clear, revealing an abundance of enriching experiences and insights that change both your perspective of the world and your position in it. The expansive benefits affect various facets of life, underscoring the immense potential found in each encounter. The following section uncovers a broad range of benefits associated with bumping dots:

- **Enhanced Authentic Connections**: Placing value on every interaction fosters genuine and meaningful connections that surpass the superficial interactions often experienced in conventional networking environments.

- **Discovery of Unexpected Opportunities**: Embracing spontaneity can open doors to unexpected and enriching opportunities, laying the groundwork for valuable personal and professional partnerships that might have otherwise gone unnoticed.

- **Personal Growth and Expansion**: Participation in diverse and unplanned interactions offers a unique platform for personal growth. It provides fresh perspectives, insights, and invaluable life lessons, enriching your personal development.

- **Increased Empathy and Understanding**: Open and curious interactions pave the way for greater empathy and understanding, nurturing harmonious, supportive, and deeper connections with others.

- **Unleashed Creativity and Innovation**: Diverse interactions act as a catalyst for creativity and innovation, inspiring new ideas, perspectives, and collaborative endeavors that drive personal and professional growth.

- **Richer Personal and Professional Networks**: While not the primary objective, bumping dots naturally augments personal and professional networks, weaving a multifaceted web of diverse and meaningful connections that enrich your life.

- **Cultivation of Openness**: Adopting this mindset encourages openness, receptivity, and adaptability.

- **Heightened Self-Awareness**: Engaging in varied and unexpected interactions can provide insights into your own preferences, values, and areas for growth, such as your interpersonal skills and emotional intelligence.

- **Improved Communication Skills**: Regular engagement with diverse individuals and scenarios challenges you to adapt your communication style, improve your ability to effectively communicate and foster stronger connections with others.

- **Greater Satisfaction and Fulfillment**: The deep and meaningful connections formed through unplanned interactions often lead to increased satisfaction and fulfillment in both personal and professional domains. These connections allow you to create a network based on mutual respect, understanding, and shared values.

- **Better Adaptability**: Regularly engaging in spontaneous and diverse interactions enhances your ability to handle uncertainty and change, leading to increased confidence.

- **Increased Resilience**: By being present in every encounter, you build the courage to never give up on engaging with others.

Each of these benefits contributes to creating a richer, more fulfilling, and more connected life, further highlighting the immense value of embracing serendipitous connections.

A Bumping Dots mindset transforms every encounter into an opportunity to find meaning and enrich the shared fabric of our humanity.

CHAPTER TWO
A Bumping Dots Mindset

As we move from the foundational concept of Bumping Dots outlined in the previous chapter, let us pivot to how one can embody this concept through a Bumping Dots mindset. If Bumping Dots is the recognition of the potential connections in our everyday interactions, then adopting a Bumping Dots mindset means to commit to the active practice of cultivating those connections. It means moving beyond the mere acknowledgment of life's spontaneous interactions and transitioning into the role of an active participant in the art of connection-building. Having grasped the notion that our lives are enriched not just by the people we seek out but also by those we stumble upon, we now explore how to intentionally bump dots.

A Bumping Dots mindset is about bringing the spirit of serendipity into every interaction. It's about creating a life where every person you meet can become a thread in the ever-expanding web of your journey, each one holding the potential to add depth, color, and texture to your world.

In this chapter, we'll delve into how to live out this concept in a way that not only enriches your life but also the lives of those around you.

At the core of a Bumping Dots mindset is a commitment to genuine openness and authenticity, which serves as the foundation for all interactions. This mindset encourages us to be fully attentive and responsive when engaging in conversations. This kind of engagement, nurtured by patience, creates a conducive environment where spontaneous and natural connections can emerge and thrive. Adopting this approach means treating every exchange as significant and approaching each interaction without preconceptions or distractions. It's about appreciating the moment for what it is and allowing the natural flow of communication to guide the connection. With authenticity at the forefront, every conversation is an opportunity to discover and respond to the authentic expressions of those around us.

With a Bumping Dots mindset, each interaction represents an opportunity to observe the natural development of chemistry and sync between people when they connect. One can also make the choice to fully participate in cultivating this rapport when it spontaneously emerges in any situation. It's not about forcing depth or seeking immediate personal gain, but rather about being present and open to the organic development of relationships. Patience plays a crucial role, allowing us to give conversations the time to unfold naturally without rushing to a conclusion or goal. Patience also enables us to be present in the interactions that fill our daily lives and to truly engage with the people we encounter in a meaningful way. Whether it's a brief chat with a neighbor or a discussion with a colleague, every moment holds the potential for something meaningful to take shape.

By embracing a Bumping Dots mindset, we transform our approach to everyday interactions. We begin to see the space around us not just as a backdrop for our daily tasks but also as a fertile ground for potential connections. This mindset calls us to release the frenzy of daily life and turn our attention to those around us. Rather than forcing relationships, we can discover vibrant bonds blossoming when we let go and interact with authenticity. By being fully present, we become aware of the nuanced intersections occurring organically in our shared spaces. When we allow things to unfold naturally, without an agenda or artifice, we can uncover the profound web of human connection already woven into our everyday world.

Seizing Serendipity

Seeking and seizing opportunities becomes about more than ambition. It shifts to being attuned to the serendipitous moments that life presents. This proactive stance involves recognizing that every encounter, no matter how brief or seemingly inconsequential, could be the doorway to a new avenue of growth, learning, or collaboration.

To adopt this facet of the Bumping Dots mindset, we must be open to possibility in all its forms. It means cultivating a sense of alertness to the potential around us and possessing a readiness to welcome new ideas, partnerships, or paths that may emerge from everyday interactions. This doesn't suggest an opportunistic approach in the traditional sense, but rather an eagerness to embrace the full spectrum of possibilities that accompany each new connection.

Living with a Bumping Dots mindset means we are constantly in a state of readiness for discovery. We understand that opportunity doesn't always knock loudly and clearly; sometimes, it's a whisper or a chance meeting that ignites a spark. It's the shared insight from a colleague over coffee, the spontaneous brainstorming session with a new acquaintance, or the mutual interest discovered during a casual conversation that could lead to exciting ventures.

To truly leverage the opportunities that a Bumping Dots mindset can uncover, we must also be willing to act. It's not enough to simply notice the potential in a connection; we must be prepared to explore it. This could mean following up on a conversation, offering your skills for a collaborative project, or even just asking more in-depth questions to understand where a synergistic relationship could lead.

Seizing the opportunities within a Bumping Dots mindset also requires a certain level of courage and initiative. It's about stepping out of our comfort zones and into the fertile ground of the unknown. It's about taking the leap to trust in the potential of a new relationship or idea, even if it's outside the scope of our current plans or expertise.

Moreover, a Bumping Dots mindset encourages us to view opportunities as two-way streets. While we may benefit from a new connection, we should also consider what we bring to the table. True opportunity is mutual; it's about creating value together, not just extracting it. This mutual exchange is what turns a chance encounter into a lasting, impactful relationship.

In essence, whether we're entrepreneurs in the traditional sense or not, a Bumping Dots mindset toward opportunities means living with an entrepreneurial spirit: being resourceful, adaptive, and enthusiastic about the potential that each new day holds. It's about cultivating a narrative of interconnected chances, understanding that the next opportunity may come from where we least expect it, and being ready to fully embrace that opportunity when it comes.

Transforming Fear and Doubt into Opportunities for Connection

A Bumping Dots mindset is not just about recognizing opportunities—it also involves overcoming the inherent fear and doubt that can accompany new interactions and the unknown paths they may lead us down. Fear and doubt are natural; they are the mind's way of cautioning us against potential risks. However, in the context of Bumping Dots, these emotions can be reframed as signals to proceed with awareness and openness rather than barriers to action.

We must learn to navigate these emotions, to recognize them when they arise, and to gently challenge them. It begins with self-awareness, understanding our own hesitations and the root causes behind them. Are we afraid of rejection, failure, or perhaps the vulnerability that comes with genuine connection? Identifying these fears is the first step toward addressing them.

Once we recognize our doubts and fears, we can start to disarm them through deliberate action. This might mean starting with small steps, like reaching out with a message to someone new or sharing an idea in a group setting, and progressively building up to more significant actions as our confidence grows. Each successful interaction, no matter how small, serves as proof that the risk of bumping dots can lead to positive outcomes, encouraging us to continue along this path.

A key aspect of overcoming fear is the cultivation of a supportive environment. Surrounding ourselves with individuals who embrace this same mindset can provide the encouragement and reassurance needed to face our fears. They can offer perspectives that challenge our doubts and celebrate our willingness to connect, even when it's difficult.

Another important strategy is to focus on the potential rewards rather than the risks, realizing that every new connection has the possibility to enrich our lives, whether through personal growth, newfound knowledge, or the joy of shared experiences. By concentrating on what we stand to gain, we can shift our mindset from one of apprehension to one of excitement about the possibilities ahead.

Practicing vulnerability is also a powerful way to conquer fear while actively seeking to bump dots. This allows us to be genuine in our interactions, creating deeper connections with others. It can be transformative, turning fear into a bridge rather than a barrier, as we find that our openness often leads to others responding kindly.

Finally, it's crucial to accept that not every interaction will lead to a significant connection, and that's okay. Part of overcoming fear and doubt is acknowledging that some dots may not lead to a direct path forward but can still add value to our experiences. Each attempt, regardless of the outcome, is a learning experience, a chance to practice resilience, and a step toward becoming more comfortable with the inherent uncertainties of life.

Through adopting a Bumping Dots mindset, we learn to see fear and doubt not as stop signs but as part of the journey. We learn to approach them with curiosity, to understand them, and to use them as catalysts for growth. This mindset becomes a powerful tool in transforming fear and doubt into guideposts, clearing the path to a life full of connections and opportunities that arise from bumping dots with the world around us.

As you live with a Bumping Dots mindset, you begin to view each interaction not just as a chance encounter but also as a doorway to new perspectives, opportunities, and friendships. This approach is about welcoming the unexpected with openness and finding joy in life's surprises. Integrating this mindset into your life means making small but significant changes in how you interact with others. Listen attentively, share your thoughts freely, and embrace the stories of those you meet. Such connections enhance your life with varied experiences, fostering empathy, creativity, and resilience. Every meeting is a chance to learn, to give, and to form connections through kindness, understanding, and interest.

To practice a Bumping Dots mindset, engage in thoughtful gestures like giving your full attention and showing genuine interest. With patience and an open mind, seek to build connections in everyday interactions. Stepping out of your comfort zone is also key. Valuing each interaction for its inherent worth and approaching each conversation with respect enriches your life and others'. When you start a new connection, invest in it with continuous care and communication, allowing it to reach its potential.

The lessons learned in this chapter open you to a world of potential friendships and relationships. These lessons move you beyond making simple introductions to developing connections and appreciating others for who they truly are. With this mindset, you can transform each day into a journey of discovery, connection, and shared growth, where every interaction presents a chance for understanding and mutual support.

Seven Daily Practices to Cultivate a Bumping Dots Mindset

Imagine moving beyond just saying hello. Think about really understanding people and sharing stories, laughter, and support. As you embark on the journey of adopting a Bumping Dots mindset, let practical steps serve as your rule of thumb. This concept requires more than understanding—it takes daily practice and conscious effort. The following seven strategies can help ingrain the essence of Bumping Dots into the core of everyday life. Committing to these actions lays the groundwork for a transformative way of living that seeks out and celebrates connection.

1. **Engage Mindfully:** Begin each day with the intention to be fully present in your interactions. This could be as simple as starting a conversation without the distraction of your phone or other devices.

2. **Listen Actively:** Make a conscious effort to listen to understand, not just to respond. Practice this by summarizing what the other person has said before adding your thoughts.

3. **Express Gratitude:** Find something to appreciate in every encounter and express your gratitude. A simple

"thank you" for someone's time or insights can go a long way.

4. **Offer Help:** Each day, look for an opportunity to assist someone else, whether it's offering guidance, support, or just a listening ear.

5. **Be Open to New Ideas:** Challenge yourself to remain open to ideas that differ from your own and consider how these perspectives can broaden your understanding.

6. **Reflect Daily:** At the end of each day, reflect on the interactions you had, what you learned from them, and how they may have expanded your viewpoint.

7. **Follow Up:** When you've had an interaction that resonates with you, take the initiative to follow up. Send a message, make a call, or schedule a meeting to continue building on that initial connection.

By incorporating these practices into your daily routine, you reinforce the principles of a Bumping Dots mindset, making it a natural part of your approach to life and relationships.

Serendipity's happy accidents transform chance encounters into meaningful connections that color the canvas of our lives.

CHAPTER THREE
The Art of Happy Accidents

The world is a grand stage of events, intertwining and overlapping, creating intricate patterns of experiences in our lives. Among these experiences, some stand out as peculiar intersections, leaving us to wonder: is this divine or is it just a random occurrence? This brings us to two fascinating concepts - coincidence and serendipity. Both might seem similar, like twins, but upon closer inspection, they have different personalities.

Coincidence can be thought of as a spontaneous alignment of events, lacking an apparent causal connection. It's like bumping into a friend at a ballgame in a city neither of you live in. Exciting, probably yes, but is it meaningful? Not necessarily. Coincidences don't always have a deeper significance, but they intrigue us because they challenge our understanding of probability.

Serendipity occurs when the Bumping Dots experiences of our lives align in such a way that the unexpected becomes a source of joy and enrichment. It's when these dots, each representing a person, collide and set in motion a series of events that unfold in surprisingly beneficial ways. When it strikes, it feels as if a divine connection is conspiring to bring you closer to your dreams or answer a question you've been pondering. It's not just about the alignment of events, but also how these events resonate with your personal quest and aspirations.

Now, how does one distinguish between the two? Think of it as turning a dial on a radio. Coincidence is when you catch snippets of a song by accident, while serendipity is when that song provides an answer or insight to something you've been mulling over. The context in which the event occurs and its alignment with your life's path or current concerns gives it meaning. Let's take a step back into the past for a moment while I recount a tale from a dot named Rick:

I was on a crowded train, lost in thought, when I spotted a wallet on the seat next to me. Being a Good Samaritan, I decided to take it to customer service. As I approached, I noticed a well-dressed man talking with one of the customer service representatives. He looked panicky and his conversation seemed intense. At this point, I'm at the service center about to hand the wallet to a customer service rep, and I hear the well-dressed gentleman say, "Oh my gosh! That's mine! Thank you so much for finding and returning it."

However, the service rep quickly grabbed the wallet and asked the gentleman his name and wanted to make sure he could properly describe the contents inside. He stated his name and began describing pictures and business cards, which led to the customer service representative returning his wallet.

The gentleman was so grateful that he offered to treat me to lunch. I agreed and we ate at a local restaurant at the train station. He thanked me again for finding and returning his wallet. During our conversation, I mentioned that I heard him tell the customer service representative that he was into film. He gave me a synopsis of his film career. I informed him that my oldest daughter was into film, and I shared some of her projects. He immediately offered to assist her and insisted that I take his phone number and have my daughter call him. The stranger that I had just met simply by returning a lost wallet turned out to be the CEO of a company that my daughter wanted to do some freelance work with.

For Rick, this twist felt like more than just a random alignment of events. It felt orchestrated, laden with purpose. That was serendipity. A chance occurrence that aligned perfectly with aspirations. In life, both coincidences and serendipitous events will sprinkle our path. While coincidences can be fun and amusing, it's the serendipitous moments that often guide us, shaping our path in ways we could never have imagined.

The Art of Noticing for Happy Accidents

The art of noticing is an invaluable tool in the quest for serendipitous experiences. It involves the skill of actively paying attention to one's surroundings while taking advantage of those unexpected and fortunate occurrences that frequently result in joyful and significant connections. By cultivating a keen sense of awareness, we prime ourselves to discover the hidden gems in our daily encounters. The art of noticing entails the following:

- **Chance Conversations:** Being observant of the little details—a unique piece of jewelry, someone's sports team apparel, or the title of the book they're engrossed in—can be the gateway to chance conversations. These small observations can serve as icebreakers, leading to exchanges that may blossom into new friendships or unexpected opportunities. It's through these observations that we find common ground with strangers, transforming mundane moments into the seeds of new relationships.

- **Sudden Insights:** Attunement to our environment can also lead to sudden insights that address lingering challenges. A designer may see a story in the chaotic dance of rain against a pane, finding inspiration for a new piece. A writer might witness the carefree flight of birds and uncover the metaphor they need to complete a poem or a story. A musician's ears might pick up a sequence of random, everyday sounds, arranging them into the foundation of a captivating new melody. These insights, while deeply personal, can also catalyze connections with others who share, appreciate, or are moved by our work.

- **Heightened Intuition:** The practice of noticing sharpens our intuition. As we become more adept at reading our environments and the people within them, we're better equipped to sense the emotional currents of situations. This heightened intuition isn't just about personal insight—it's also a social tool that enhances our empathy, allowing us to connect more deeply and navigate social interactions with greater understanding and finesse.

- **The Rhythm of the World:** Incorporating the art of noticing into our daily lives harmonizes our rhythm with that of the world around us. As our awareness expands, so does the likelihood of encountering these happy accidents. They become more than just coincidental occurrences; they are moments ripe with potential, waiting for us to unlock them. This increased frequency of serendipitous moments enhances our lives, adding layers of depth and color to our everyday experiences.

By mastering the art of noticing, we don't just live in the world—we engage with it actively, drawing out the diverse array of connections and opportunities that it has to offer. In this way, we turn the art of noticing into a way of life, one where every moment is an opportunity for a beautiful and happy accident.

Benchside Revelations

Several years ago, on a sunlit spring afternoon, I had some time to spare before my next graduate class at the University of Missouri-Columbia (Mizzou). I chose a bench near Jesse Hall to relax and soak in the ambiance. As I neared the bench, a gentleman, who looked to be in his late forties or early fifties, was already seated, deeply engrossed in a book. With a friendly nod, I introduced myself and took a seat.

He reciprocated the gesture, revealing his first name and the title of the book he was reading. What started as a simple discussion about the book's themes seamlessly shifted into a captivating conversation about the city of Columbia's rich history and the storied legacy of the University of Missouri. For over half an hour, we exchanged anecdotes and insights, each moment reinforcing the beauty of unplanned interactions.

As the hands of the clock edged towards my class time, I stood up to leave. After exchanging farewells, I began my walk to class. During this walk, an acquaintance from the university stopped me. "Do you know who you were just talking to?" they inquired. I confessed my ignorance, only to learn that the gentleman was an heir to the Walton family legacy, as in Sam Walton, the visionary behind Walmart.

That spontaneous conversation by Jesse Hall was not just about learning more about Columbia or Mizzou; it was a testament to life's unpredictability. Not only did I get to hear fascinating tales about the city and university, but I also received life insights from someone who came from a legacy of immense influence and success. This serendipitous meeting was merely one of the many unexpected twists that life had in store for me.

Life is replete with moments where unexpected encounters transform into memorable stories or lessons learned. These chance interactions often happen when we least expect them but can leave a profound impact. However, while we cannot control serendipity, we can certainly create an environment conducive to such moments. By cultivating certain habits and perspectives and applying the strategies below, we can increase our likelihood of experiencing enriching chance encounters.

- **Practice Mindfulness:** It's more than a buzzword. Being fully present in a moment, aware of where you are and what you are doing, even if it's just waiting in line at the coffee shop, can lead to unexpected conversations and connections.

- **Challenge Yourself:** Every week, try something new. A new restaurant, a new hobby class, or a new podcast. Diverse experiences often lead to diverse interactions.

- **Celebrate Stories:** When someone shares a tale or a snippet from their life, cherish it. Every story offers a new lens to view the world.

- **Share Without Expectation:** It's not always about gaining. Sometimes, sharing a kind word, an anecdote, or even a book recommendation can make someone's day.

- **Initiate:** If you feel a nudge to compliment someone or start a conversation, act on it. These small impulses can lead to memorable interactions.

- **Document the Journey:** Consider maintaining a journal, not of the everyday happenings, but of those unexpected moments, surprising conversations, and the feelings they evoked. Over time, you'll have a repository of beautiful memories that capture how you've grown in the art of noticing.

So, as you step out today, look around with renewed enthusiasm, and embrace the countless possibilities life presents. Keep in mind that every person you meet holds the potential to add a new, unexpected, beautiful chapter to your life.

Intuition in connections is like a compass for the soul, guiding us to recognize our dots—those special people with whom our spirits resonate. It's a dance of instinct and insight, leading us to connections that are not just encounters but also profound alignments of our paths.

CHAPTER FOUR

Intuition in Connections: Recognizing Your Dots

Have you ever played with one of those kids toys where you're trying to fit different shapes into their matching holes? Imagine, for a moment, that each interaction with someone new is like trying to bump two shapes together. This process is unseen, made of intangible feelings, intuitions, vibes if you will. Sometimes the shapes, or "dots," just don't fit no matter how hard you try to push them together. At other times, they click perfectly without effort.

Our instincts, often described as a "gut feeling," act as our internal shape or dot recognizer. They are a legacy from our evolutionary past, developed to help us react quickly to situations - whether that be a saber-toothed tiger lurking in the shadows or a potential ally from another tribe. Our brain, in moments often too fleeting for us to consciously notice, picks up signals and analyzes them based on memories, past lessons, and even biological reactions.

Think back to the initial moments of meeting someone. Did you ever get an immediate vibe, a feeling that told you "I'm going to get along with this person?" Conversely, have you met someone and felt wary, without even knowing why? That's your intuition working. It's the unseen process of dots trying to find a fit.

Several years ago, while deeply engaged with a book at a local bookstore, I was approached by a stranger, Sara, who initiated a dialogue about the material I was reading. Many of us have experienced these brief exchanges with acquaintances—cordial, yet typically inconsequential. With Sara, however, the dynamic was unique. Our ideas and perspectives didn't just meet; they resonated with a rare synergy. Our conversation was effortless, marked by a mutual understanding that is hard to articulate. A few months later, driven by a shared vision and mutual trust in our professional judgment, Sara and I decided to pursue a joint venture. This decision led to a fruitful business partnership, and beyond that, a valued professional ally and friend.

Upon reflection, I realized I could have easily overlooked our initial interaction as just another routine conversation. Yet, by heeding my instincts, I welcomed an opportunity for a profound professional relationship. It stands as a testament to the power of intuition to recognize potential where the eye might overlook.

Deeper Dive into Intuition

Intuition is our inner wisdom and gut feelings that arise without conscious reasoning. At its core, it is an effortless, quick, and automatic experience that arises in response to a situation or problem. It's the mind's way of using deep-seated knowledge and experiences to inform actions or decisions without the individual being fully aware of the underlying reasons for their choice. Intuition can provide useful insights and guide our decision-making. However, it is important to find a balance in how we understand and use intuition.

On one hand, completely ignoring intuition discounts our deeper knowledge. Our logical reasoning also has blind spots, so input from our intuitive voice provides an important complementary perspective. We may miss out on opportunities or insights if we don't listen to our intuitive nudges. On the other hand, relying entirely on intuition without objective analysis can lead us astray. Intuition may stem from biased memories or be swayed by recent emotions rather than the full scope of knowledge. It's important to consciously evaluate the soundness of intuitive perspectives before acting on them.

A balanced approach involves listening to intuition as an input but not as the final word. We can pay attention to messages from our subconscious but then analyze them rationally. If intuition aligns with reason, we can act on it more confidently. If not, more contemplation may be needed.

Our personal values, identity, and self-trust also play a role. Intuition that aligns with our core values is more likely to be trustworthy than fleeting impulses. Connecting with our true self can help filter intuitive insights. Having faith in our own inner wisdom, while still questioning it, allows us to integrate intuition more effectively.

With practice, we can get better at recognizing when to tap into intuition, and when to supplement it with additional critical thinking. The key is keeping intuition integrated as part of a thoughtful decision process, rather than either overriding logic or being overridden by it. Together, our inner wisdom (intuition) and outer wisdom (logic) can guide us more powerfully than either alone. By learning to listen to intuition while also scrutinizing it, we can achieve a healthy balance that leverages the full strengths of our mind.

Practices to Hone Your Intuitive Skills

Our intuition, much like any skill, can be sharpened and refined. Think of it as leading your personal dot (you) to make more meaningful bumps and connections. Here are some practices to help you navigate the vast space of experiences and feelings, allowing your intuitive dot to bump and connect more effectively:

1. **Mindfulness Practice**: Cultivating mindfulness through meditation or other relaxation techniques can help quiet the noise of the mind, allowing the subtle voice of intuition to be heard. It's about being present in the moment and attentive to the impulses and sensations that arise.

2. **Reflective Journaling:** Keeping a journal can be a useful tool to track intuitive hits and misses. Over time, patterns may emerge, which can provide insights into how your intuition communicates with you.

3. **Body Awareness:** The body often exhibits physical responses when intuition strikes. A sense of comfort or discomfort, "butterflies" in the stomach, or a feeling of restlessness could all be indicators. Tuning into these bodily sensations can serve as a guide.

4. **Emotional Literacy:** Being in touch with your emotions allows you to differentiate between fear-based reactions and true intuitive knowledge. Intuition

often feels neutral or calm, even when it's steering you away from something.

5. **Openness to Experience:** Imagine a dot that only moves within a limited space; its bumps and connections will be limited. By being open to new experiences and viewpoints, you're giving your dot - your intuition - a broader playing field with more potential bumps and connections that could lead to richer insights. This broadens the database your subconscious has to draw from, potentially making your intuitive insights more comprehensive and accurate.

6. **Balanced Skepticism:** While intuition can be incredibly powerful, it's important to balance it with rational thought. Consider your intuitive feelings as one aspect of the decision-making process, not the sole determinant.

7. **The Search for Confirmation:** Where possible, look for empirical evidence to support your intuitive decisions. Confirmation can come from external sources or from a sense of internal alignment and congruence.

Remember, intuition isn't about always being right but rather about trusting your personal journey as a dot, including the bumps, the misses, and the beautiful connections you make along the way. With practice, you can form more meaningful connections, enhancing not just your intuitive skills but also your life experiences.

Intuition acts as a silent guide when engaging with those individuals who could potentially be our dots—the people with whom we share an intrinsic connection. It informs our recognition of serendipitous moments and guides the flow of our interactions surrounding these special connections. The following are examples of these processes.

Using Intuition to Recognize Serendipitous Moments:

1. **Sense of Right Timing:** Intuition can signal when a chance meeting with a dot is more than a coincidence. It's an internal nod that the timing is for a reason, perhaps to catalyze an important idea or decision.

2. **Feeling of Significance:** Even ordinary moments can feel laden with significance when experienced with your dots. Intuition can amplify this sensation, suggesting a deeper meaning or opportunity within the encounter.

3. **Alignment of Circumstances:** Intuition helps recognize when circumstances align in a way that benefits your connection with a dot. This might include unexpected opportunities to collaborate or support each other.

4. **Inspiration to Act:** Intuition can inspire spontaneous actions with that might seem strange at the moment but lead to serendipitous outcomes, like an impromptu meeting that turns into a creative brainstorming session.

5. **Recognition of Growth Opportunities:** Intuition can reveal that a moment shared with a dot is ripe for personal or professional growth, urging you to seize the opportunity presented by this synergistic relationship.

Using Intuition to Guide Conversations:

1. **Harmonizing Communication:** Intuition can help synchronize your communication with a dot. It guides the rhythm of the conversation, often prompting when to probe deeper or when to provide space.

2. **Anticipating Needs:** You might intuitively anticipate what a dot might say or need in a conversation, leading

to a deeply empathetic exchange that feels both fluid and intuitive.

3. **Understanding the Unspoken:** Intuition often allows for a level of unspoken understanding with a dot. You may find yourselves finishing each other's sentences or picking up on subtleties that outsiders might miss.

4. **Navigating Conflict:** When disagreements arise, intuition can help navigate the conversation towards resolution, sensing the underlying issues and guiding the dialogue to address them.

5. **Affirming Connections:** Intuitive feelings during a conversation can often reaffirm your connection with a dot, making the interaction more meaningful. In essence, intuition acts as a guide and a connector, deepening the conversations and experiences shared with our dots. It's the thread that weaves through the fabric of these relationships, highlighting moments of serendipity and synchronicity that might otherwise go unnoticed. By trusting and acting on our intuitive insights, we can enrich these connections, making the most of the unique alignment we share with these individuals.

Using Intuition to Recognize Your Dots

Recognizing whether someone is your dot—a person with whom you share a profound connection or whose values and intuition align with yours—can often be discerned through several intuitive clues:

1. **Immediate Resonance:** When you meet someone who is your dot, there's often an instant sense of familiarity or comfort. It's an intuitive nudge that this person fits into your life's puzzle effortlessly.

2. **Ease of Communication:** With a true dot, conversations flow naturally. You may find that you're on the same wavelength, often understanding each other without needing to elaborate extensively.

3. **Shared Values:** Intuition can signal a dot through the recognition of shared core values and beliefs. There's a deep-seated sense that your foundational principles align.

4. **Mutual Understanding:** Even with minimal interaction, there's a profound understanding of each other's perspectives and feelings. It feels as though your internal dots are in sync.

5. **Authenticity:** There's a sense of authenticity when you're with someone who is your dot. You can be your true self without pretense, and your intuition confirms the genuineness of the connection.

6. **Consistent Energy:** The energy between you and a true dot remains consistent. It's a person who energizes rather than drains you, and this is something you can intuitively feel.

7. **Trust and Reliability:** Your intuition might hint that someone is your dot if there's an inherent trust and you find them reliable. It's a subconscious recognition of their consistent behavior that resonates with your inner expectations.

8. **Positive Impact:** Notice the impact that someone has on you. Your dot typically leaves you feeling uplifted and supported, guiding you towards growth and positivity.

9. **Sense of Belonging:** With your dot, there's a strong sense of belonging. Intuition often guides this feeling, suggesting a deep-rooted connection.

10. **Harmony in Differences:** Even when there are differences, with a true dot, there's a harmonious balance. Your intuition can detect when these differences complement each other rather than create discord.

Intuition in discerning dots often involves a complex interplay of emotional responses, bodily sensations, and spontaneous recognition. It's about trusting those subtle internal signals that suggest when you're in the presence of someone who inherently understands and connects with your innermost self. If a dot or potential connection does not align with the intuitive clues above, this may be a sign that this is not the dot for you.

Using Intuition to Reflect on Your Dots

Reflection is a crucial step in understanding the depth of your intuitive abilities and the patterns of your interactions. Here are questions intended to lead you on this introspective journey to assess how you can best bump dots.

Recall a Recent Interaction:
- Describe a recent interaction where you felt a strong intuitive nudge.
- Did you follow it?
- If you didn't follow it, why?
- If you did follow it, what was the outcome?

Analyze Your Comfort Zone:

- What new experiences have you engaged in recently?
- Why did you choose these experiences to engage in?
- How did these experiences influence your intuitive feelings and dot connections?

Assess Your Attention to Intuition:

- On a scale from 1 to 10, with 10 being the greatest, how much attention do you pay to your intuitive feelings in daily interactions?
- Why do you think the number you chose is accurate?

Evaluate Outcomes:

- Reflect on a situation where you trusted your intuition. What was the result?
- On the flip side, consider a scenario where you ignored your intuition. What was the result? What insights did you gain?

Future Commitments:

- Detail how you will commit to honing your intuitive skills moving forward. List three actionable steps.

Embrace this space of self-reflection. It is important to periodically refer to this section as you navigate your way through your Bumping Dots experiences. Witness your growth, note the changes, and watch your evolution unfold. This reflective exercise is your companion, ensuring you traverse this path with heightened awareness, profound understanding, and a resolute commitment to personal and intuitive growth.

When we are vulnerable with the dots in our lives, it is like unlocking a hidden door to our inner world, where our most authentic selves reside. Our vulnerability invites others to step in and connect with us on a level that transcends the ordinary, creating ties that are as deeply meaningful as they are genuine.

CHAPTER FIVE

Embracing Vulnerability
With Other Dots

We've explored how the unexpected moments in life often shape us more profoundly than the meticulously planned ones. It's in the unplanned, the unforeseen, and the spontaneous where we truly meet ourselves. Vulnerability is the currency of these moments. To share authentically is to present oneself, thoughts, feelings, and experiences without a facade. It means removing the mask we often wear to fit into societal norms or to protect ourselves from potential judgment. It's about being genuine and honest, both with oneself and with others. But why is this such a daunting task for many of us? Well, to be authentic means exposing parts of oneself that are often kept hidden, and that comes with both risks and rewards.

Perhaps the most daunting risk is the potential for judgment and criticism. When you open up and reveal your authentic self, there's always a vulnerability to the judgments of others. This fear, rooted in the apprehension of not being accepted or understood, often acts as a barrier to real self-expression within the realm of Bumping Dots.

Another significant risk tied to authenticity is the fear of rejection. Authenticity may require unveiling aspects of us that are not typically accepted or embraced. In doing so, there's always the possibility that someone may disagree with or fail to comprehend our perspective, leading to feelings of rejection or exclusion. This fear of not fitting in or of being rejected for who we truly are can be an influential deterrent, casting a shadow over our serendipitous interactions and keeping us from being present.

Furthermore, there's the risk of exposure. Sharing deeply personal stories or emotions can leave us feeling emotionally exposed in front of others. This fear stems from the idea of granting someone else the power to potentially hurt us by revealing our vulnerabilities. It's a risk that often keeps us guarded in our interactions, preventing us from fully embracing the beauty of bumping dots.

Misunderstandings also pose a challenge when we engage in authentic sharing within the context of serendipitous encounters. While our intentions may be good, there's a risk that our truths can be taken out of context or misunderstood, leading to unintended complications or conflicts. This risk underscores the importance of clear and effective communication when sharing our authentic selves in these moments of serendipity.

In navigating these risks, individuals must strike a balance between self-expression and self-protection. Authenticity can be a beautiful and transformative force within the world of Bumping Dots, but it requires careful consideration of these potential pitfalls. Recognizing these risks and finding ways to mitigate them can empower individuals to share their authentic selves with greater confidence and resilience, enhancing their experiences within the serendipitous world of Bumping Dots.

Rewards of Authentic Sharing in the World of Bumping Dots

Despite the risks and vulnerabilities that accompany authentic sharing, the rewards are profound and far-reaching, enriching both personal and interpersonal experiences. Primarily among these rewards is the cultivation of genuine connections. When you embrace authenticity within the world of Bumping Dots, you naturally draw like-minded individuals towards you. These connections, built upon a foundation of truth and transparency, are inherently more profound and meaningful. They foster a sense of belonging and camaraderie that resonates on a deeper level, enhancing the serendipitous beauty of each interaction.

Authentic sharing also serves as a catalyst for personal growth. Confronting the fears and vulnerabilities associated with authenticity can lead to profound personal development. It nurtures self-awareness and self-acceptance, allowing individuals to evolve and become more in tune with their true selves. This personal growth not only enhances individual experiences within Bumping Dots but also contributes to the positive evolution of the collective interactions.

Trust building is another invaluable reward of authenticity within Bumping Dots. Authenticity serves as a cornerstone of trust. When you are genuine, people tend to trust you more readily. This trust, whether in personal or professional relationships, lays the groundwork for stronger and more resilient connections, amplifying the positive impact of serendipitous encounters.

In the realm of personal liberation, authentic sharing bestows a unique sense of freedom. The burden of upholding a facade or concealing one's true self is lifted, liberating individuals from the exhausting effort of maintaining an inauthentic persona. This newfound freedom allows them to engage in more purposeful pursuits and experiences within the world of Bumping Dots.

Moreover, the power of authenticity extends to empowerment, both for oneself and others. Each instance of authentic sharing serves as an inspiration and a source of courage. It empowers not only the individual sharing their truth but also those who witness it. It sends a powerful message that it is okay to be real, to be vulnerable, and to embrace one's authentic self within the ever-evolving dance of Bumping Dots.

Herb's Moment of Vulnerability During Open Mic Night

One winter season, our family embarked on a cruise. The vibrant energy of the ship instantly set the stage for a memorable vacation. One of the standout features of our voyage was the nightly entertainment, and at the heart of it all was Mickey, a guest comedian who quickly became the talk of the ship.

While heading to lunch, my family and I crossed paths with Mickey. What could have been a passing exchange of greetings led to us sitting together. As the meal unfolded, so did our conversations, making the lunch a genuine session of bumping dots. We connected over shared stories and empathized with life's challenges. Mickey poured out tales from his life, weaving in his dreams and detailing the rollercoaster ride of his career in comedy.

Feeling inspired by his candor, I let down my guard and admitted a long-held dream of mine: to experience the thrill of an open mic night, standing under the spotlight and evoking laughter. Later that evening, as we settled into our seats for Mickey's performance, I expected nothing more than a night filled with hearty laughter. But, as his set ended, Mickey announced, "Folks, I've got a surprise guest for you tonight!" The spotlight shifted to me, and the room grew silent. I was taken aback, feeling utterly unprepared, and faced with hundreds of expectant eyes.

As I walked towards the stage, gulping down my nervousness, I remembered our lunchtime conversation, pulling jokes and anecdotes we'd shared. As I began, the room's atmosphere changed from anticipation to chuckles, then full-blown laughter. By the end of my impromptu act, a standing ovation greeted me, an experience both humbling and exhilarating.

For the remainder of our cruise, I was no longer just another passenger. People approached for photos and lauded my surprise performance, and a cruise staff member even expressed interest in having me open for another comedy show. From a casual lunchtime confession, my vulnerability transported me to a once-in-a-lifetime adventure. The message was evident: when we embrace vulnerability, life has a way of surprising us with rewards we'd never imagined.

While the risks of sharing authentically can be intimidating, the rewards are rich. Every interaction and every relationship becomes an opportunity for deeper connection and growth. By understanding and weighing these risks and rewards, one can make informed choices about when, where, and how to share authentically. In doing so, we pave the way for a life filled with genuine relationships, personal growth, and true fulfillment.

The Transformative Effects of Vulnerability

Vulnerability serves as an honest icebreaker. So often, we engage in superficial small talk when meeting new people, a habit that rarely leads to meaningful connection. However, when we summon the courage to share our vulnerabilities, we break through the surface and dive into sincere conversations. That pivotal moment when we admit a fear, an insecurity, or a past mistake can act as a catalyst, propelling us into fresh connections that would have otherwise remained uncharted.

Perhaps most remarkably, vulnerability has the potential to transform strangers into confidantes. Sharing a personal story, especially one that exposes our vulnerabilities, is an act of trust—an invitation for others to reciprocate. These exchanges of vulnerability lay the foundation for friendships steeped in trust, understanding, and shared experiences. Furthermore, vulnerability is a catalyst for growth and healing, not only in our relationships with others but also within ourselves. Being open about our struggles and challenges allows us to acknowledge them and begin to overcome them. The support and guidance we receive from those with whom we connect can be a guiding light on our path to becoming stronger and more resilient individuals.

While our lives are often defined by our hustles and facades, our vulnerabilities hold a secret treasure. Moments of unguarded and unfiltered expressions allow us to create meaningful connections. Vulnerability possesses a remarkable power: it paves the way for connections that are far from ordinary. By sharing our fears, insecurities, and dreams, we grant others the gift of permission to do the same, creating bonds that are deeply rooted in pure human connection.

Unexpected Possibilities through Herb's Vulnerability with a Friend

After my college graduation, I found myself employed as a correctional officer, working a demanding shift that left little room to savor life's offerings, including spending time with my wife Christine and our older daughter Ashley, who was a baby at the time. On top of that, I was at a crossroads with no clear direction for my next career move. All I knew was that the path of being a correctional officer wasn't the one I wanted to continue. I needed a fresh start!

In the midst of my pondering, my phone rang. It was a call from my fraternity brother Mark, a man highly respected and synonymous with triumph in my eyes. Despite being just two years older than me, Mark exuded wisdom and insight that felt light-years beyond our peers. His natural leadership qualities and strong academic acumen made his advice invaluable.

As I answered the call, Mark's warm and familiar voice cut through the dim glow of my apartment. He noticed the despondency in my tone and with genuine concern said, "You seem dejected." In the intimate confines of our conversation, an impulse to confide in him overcame me. I confessed, "I'm stuck in a stressful job that I despise, and I have no idea where to go from here."

Mark's attentive silence on the other end of the line encouraged me to continue. When I had laid bare my fears, he responded in a smooth but confident tone, "I know it wasn't easy for you to share that with me, but I'm glad you did." Mark then posed a question that would change the course of my life. He asked, "Have you ever considered graduate school?" I admitted that the thought hadn't really crossed my mind, given my family responsibilities at the time.

Mark informed me that he was on the brink of applying to graduate school himself and began to passionately advocate for the benefits of pursuing an advanced degree. He offered his unwavering support and said, "We can embark on this journey together, and I'll assist you in any way I can." As he painted a vivid picture of the potential academic and personal rewards, it wasn't just the idea of graduate school that stuck with me; it was the profound realization that sometimes opening up about our fears can lead to unexpected solutions.

The dialogue with Mark proved to be a turning point in my life. It not only unveiled the potential path of advanced studies but also illuminated the profound strength rooted in vulnerability. By sharing my doubts with someone I held in high regard, I was met with insight and a sharpened perspective moving forward.

Post-graduation life wasn't confined to the pursuit of additional degrees; it stood as a tribute to the power unearthed in embracing vulnerability and actively seeking advice. This chapter of my life also unfurled a wealth of opportunities and paved the way for my continued doctoral endeavors. All these incredible advancements stemmed from a willingness to be present, vulnerable, and open to the many possibilities' life presented.

Exercises to Foster Vulnerability within the World of Bumping Dots

Becoming the best version of ourselves is not always a straight path; it's one that requires us to step beyond our comfort zones. Our comfort zone, while familiar and reassuring, can also limit our potential for new experiences and self-discovery. In the spirit of embracing the concept of Bumping Dots, this section offers a set of exercises that gently nudge you beyond your comfort zone into vulnerability.

- **The "I Am" Exercise: Revealing the Unspoken** - On a sheet of paper, write down five sentences that start with "I am..." These should be aspects of yourself that you rarely express. This exercise is all about self-awareness and vulnerability. Sharing these truths during serendipitous encounters fosters a deeper understanding of who you are and allows others to connect with the real you. It transforms ordinary interactions into profound moments of connection, where dots resonate with each other's authentic selves.

- **Deep Dive: Beyond the Surface** - The next time you find yourself in a discussion, challenge yourself to go beyond the usual small talk. Ask questions that invite thoughtful responses. When you engage in meaningful conversations with others during serendipitous encounters, you open the door to genuine connections and opportunities. By sharing your authentic thoughts, you create an atmosphere where dots can connect on a deeper level.

- **The Vulnerability Challenge: Embracing the Unfamiliar** - Think about something you've always wanted to do but have held back due to self-consciousness or fear. It could be singing at a karaoke bar, joining a dance class, or even writing a personal essay. Embrace the vulnerability that comes with trying something new and notice how it feels to be both vulnerable and alive. Conquering the fear of the unfamiliar during serendipitous encounters allows you to fully engage in the moment. It transforms potentially mundane interactions into adventures, where dots connect through shared experiences and bold vulnerability.

These exercises were designed to gently push you out of your comfort zone. Embracing vulnerability isn't about recklessly exposing ourselves to harm. It's about choosing to be authentic, even when it's uncomfortable, because that's where true connections happen.

A life filled with bumped dots is far more interesting than one that's just a straight line. So, let's be courageous in showing our true selves. Now, you're not just bumping into dots; you're connecting them in a way that paints a fuller, richer picture of who you are and what your life can be.

An essential yet overlooked skill when bumping dots is knowing when connections aren't meant to be. At times, we must navigate away from encounters, preserving energy for likeminded dots - those destined to resonate at our core.

CHAPTER SIX

WHO'S NOT YOUR DOT?

Every chance meeting and serendipitous encounter doesn't always bloom into a meaningful connection. Understanding this is pivotal, and it's crucial to recognize when to step back, ensuring such moments do not deplete our energy or self-esteem. I've lived this lesson, and it's a story I hold close as a gentle reminder of the unpredictable dance of connections.

On a particular trip with my older daughter, we were enroute to an illustrious event teeming with actors, actresses, screenwriters, and directors. Amid one of the sessions, I found myself in delightful conversations with several individuals. Eagerly, I shared a snippet about my daughter's budding film career, fervent passion, and recent debut.

As a father beaming with pride, I was oblivious to the subtle signs of disinterest from one individual. His demeanor didn't register until my daughter later joined us, unaware of the conversation we had just had. As she echoed my sentiments about her background, he cut her off. He abruptly spoke the words "Your dad has already shared who you are" in a tone laden with impatience. It dawned upon me that his perception was clouded, perhaps assuming we sought some favor or had some expectations from him.

In that moment, the realization hit hard: not all chance meetings would flourish beyond a mere hello and goodbye. This experience didn't mar my spirit. Instead, it bolstered my understanding of the fragile nature of serendipitous interactions.

Reflecting upon this, I felt an urge to share this insight in my book. This experience aided my navigation through the complexities of life's encounters. I understood the importance of identifying someone who was not my dot. In situations akin to my experience, it's crucial to assess the other person's openness to the interaction. Recognize the signs of disinterest or discomfort and allow yourself the grace to exit the situation without internalizing the outcome. Overcoming the allure of a potentially fruitful connection is a challenging yet essential skill. Trust your intuition to guide you, and remember, not every connection is meant to be nurtured. When met with abruptness or disinterest like I experienced, remind yourself to maintain respect and courtesy as you gracefully exit the interaction. It's not a reflection of your worth but merely the nature of human dynamics.

Post-departure, engage in reflection to process the experience fully. In my case, I learned valuable lessons. It reinforced the understanding that every encounter carries the seed of learning, contributing to personal growth and polishing the ability to build meaningful connections. The act of reflecting will provide clarity, closure, and insights for future interactions. It's not about taking each interaction personally but about learning, growing, and continuously improving your skills in navigating the world of serendipitous encounters.

Identifying Misaligned Dots

Consider my story when I traveled with my daughter to a prominent event filled with notable individuals from the film industry. It's essential to notice such signs early to maintain emotional well-being. Here are some signs to identify misaligned dots:

- **Feel the Emotional Climate:** Pay attention to continuous uneasiness. If discomfort overshadows your interactions, it's a hint of a misaligned connection. Just like my encounter at the event, the abrupt and uninterested response was a clear signal.

- **Assess Your Energy Levels:** A beneficial connection will energize you, not deplete your spirit. If you consistently feel exhausted after interactions, it's a sign to reevaluate. Connections should uplift, not drag you down.

- **Observe the Balance:** A one-sided relationship, where the efforts and investments tilt heavily to one side, isn't fruitful. Like a balanced seesaw, both sides should have balanced input and reciprocal appreciation.

- **Seek Growth:** Look for mutual growth and learning in each interaction. If those are absent and things seem stagnant, it's a sign to assess the connection's real value.

- **Commit to Regular Self-Assessments:** Make self-assessments a consistent practice. Reflect on your connections' impact on your well-being, happiness, and life progress. This routine will aid in ensuring your social circle is vibrant and supportive and positively contributes to your life.

By learning to identify misaligned dots, we enhance our ability to navigate the complexities of relationships, ensuring our energy and time are invested in connections that genuinely nourish and uplift us.

Overcoming the Draw of Serendipity

Imagine attending a book club meeting. The anticipation of sharing thoughts and lively discussions about a recently read book is exhilarating. At the meeting, a sudden introduction to a fellow book lover happens. Discussions flow effortlessly, and the connection feels promising. However, as weeks progress, conversations that were once vibrant and intellectually stimulating turn monotonous and draining. The initial attraction of this serendipitous connection dims as it doesn't contribute positively to your personal growth or well-being. Below, we will discuss how you must challenge the charm, trust your intuition, and possibly consult your inner circle to determine if this is a dot you should continue to bump with.

- **Challenge the Charm:** Learn from the situation above with the book club meeting. Review your connections objectively. Beyond the initial shared interests and engaging conversations, does this connection enhance your life, impart knowledge, or bring joy? If not, it might not be as valuable as it seemed at first glance.

- **Trust Your Intuition:** As the conversations turn monotonous, pay attention to your feelings. If you find

- yourself dreading the discussions or feeling drained post interaction, it's your intuition signaling that this connection may not be worthwhile.

- **Consult Your Inner Circle:** Don't hesitate to seek advice from friends or family. Share your feelings about the change in dynamics and listen to their perspectives. An outsider's view can sometimes provide the insight needed to make an informed decision about continuing or gracefully exiting the connection.

Learning to recognize when it's necessary to disengage from unsuitable connections, and doing so with respect, enables you to move forward confidently and compassionately. Should you decide that it's time to step away from a connection, here are some ways to navigate that transition:

- **Plan Your Departure:** Reflect on the reasons this connection doesn't serve your professional or personal growth. Be straightforward in acknowledging this to yourself. When it's time to communicate this to the other person, choose your words wisely to maintain professionalism and respect.

- **Be Honest Yet Polite:** Express your feelings and concerns calmly and respectfully. If necessary, explain why you think it's best to part ways and emphasize the mutual respect you wish to maintain.

- **Practice Clear Communication:** Preparation is key when it comes to making your decision. Write down your thoughts and practice your words to ensure your message is articulate and compassionate. This careful approach helps in maintaining a courteous tone, ensuring the departure is considerate of both parties and as smooth as possible.

Reflection After Moving Away from a Connection

Moving away from a connection is a significant step, so it's crucial to spend time reflecting after departure. This reflection will assist in understanding the interaction's impact and will help prevent similar issues in the future.

- **Evaluate the Experience:** What were the signs that there was a shift in the fruitful nature of the connection? What can you learn from this experience that can help you in the future?

- **Future Interaction Insights:** Use this time to garner insights for future relationships. Understand what worked and what didn't in this connection to better navigate future interactions.

The clarity gained from reflection is paramount, not just for achieving closure but also for equipping you with crucial insights that will be instrumental in managing and assessing your future connections. Such reflective practices contribute significantly to personal growth and lay a solid foundation for the establishment of future connections that are healthy and mutually beneficial.

While bumping dots, we can foster self-discovery and growth by discerning which connections to nurture and which to let go. If there is a lesson to be learned or a lasting connection to be built, let us embrace the understanding that every encounter holds value. We should not view the end of a connection as a failure but as a chance to refine our interpersonal skills and enhance our emotional intelligence. Be confident in your intuition, respect your emotional well-being, and honor the dignity of others. Throughout our multifaceted paths, may we carry the wisdom to navigate the intricate web of connections with grace, empathy, and clarity, always keeping in mind that everyone we encounter has a unique place in our life's story.

In Bumping Dots, getting to know someone is like exploring a map full of interesting places. Each person is a new, exciting destination, and our journey is about discovering and appreciating the unique qualities of every spot we visit.

CHAPTER SEVEN
Understanding Personalities

In the bright and varied world of personalities, my family is a vivid patchwork quilt. Each square tells a different story, each color represents a unique disposition, and each pattern depicts individual traits, yet all are seamlessly stitched together with threads of love, respect, and understanding.

When people first meet my family, especially when we're out and about or on vacation, they immediately notice the lively chatter and boundless energy radiating from me and my younger daughter Kimberly. We're like two peas in a pod, both extroverted and always ready to make a new friend, share a fascinating story, and fill every room with laughter and warmth.

Conversely, providing a gentle and soothing balance to our lively duo, my wife Christine and our older daughter Ashley are the quiet and observant ones in the patchwork. They walk the world with softer steps, cherishing one-on-one interactions and the tranquil strum of a peaceful evening. They are the cool, calming blues to our vibrant reds, providing depth and balance to our family's dynamic spectrum. Beyond the public gaze, the doors of our home open to a symphony of diverse notes. It's a harmonious scene filled with the lively conversation where everyone's social side, even Christine's and Ashley's, comes to life. In the comfort of our home, the conversations flow like a gentle river, affirming the strength of our familial bonds.

Bumping Dots synchronizes our varying personalities harmoniously. At the grocery store or any social setting, I find joy in engaging with multiple individuals and leaving with a host of new acquaintances. Christine and Ashley, with their gentle grace, may choose to intimately connect with a solitary soul, creating bonds that are deep, sincere, and lasting.

Despite our different personalities, we have cultivated a keen awareness of each other's social boundaries. There's a humorous and familiar scenario where Christine gracefully bows out from a gathering or a conversation, signaling her time to retreat and rejuvenate and leaving me to carry on the jovial exchanges. This mutual respect for personal boundaries and capacities ensures a balance within our lively clan, where everyone's comfort and preferences are upheld with utmost respect and consideration.

Personality refers to the unique combination of characteristics, behaviors, and patterns of thought that define an individual and differentiate them from others. These traits include emotional responses, social interactions, and a host of other patterns of behavior that emerge from early childhood and continue throughout life. Personality is not static; it evolves as people grow and encounter different life experiences. It's not a label or a box that confines someone to specific behaviors or reactions. It's also not an indicator of value, meaning one type of personality is not superior or inferior to another. Each personality type has its unique strengths and potential areas for growth.

The idea of personality spectrums isn't new. Eysenck (1967) noted that personalities range on a continuum from introverted to extroverted.[1] While introverts tend to feel more comfortable in solitary or low-stimulus environments, extroverts thrive in more socially engaging situations. Later, the Myers-Briggs Type Indicator (MBTI) expanded on this, classifying personalities into 16 types based on four dichotomies, including the introversion-extroversion spectrum.[2]

---

[1] Eysenck, H. J. (1967). The biological basis of personality. Transaction Publishers.

[2] Myers, I. B., & McCaulley, M. H. (1985). Manual: A guide to the development and use of the Myers-Briggs Type Indicator. Consulting Psychologists Press.

Introverts

Introverts are individuals who often feel more comfortable and energized in solitary or small group settings. They may find large social gatherings draining, preferring to spend time alone to recharge. Introverts often enjoy activities that allow for deep thought and reflection. However, being introverted does not mean a person is shy or unsocial; they simply have different social preferences and energy management.

Extroverts

Extroverts are individuals who thrive in social settings. They feel energized by interacting with others and often seek out social opportunities. Extroverts tend to enjoy group activities and community environments. Being an extrovert does not mean a person is incapable of enjoying solitude or that they are always outgoing and loud; they just generally prefer more social interaction.

Understanding the basic distinction between introverts and extroverts is just the tip of the iceberg. Each category can be further divided into various personality types, each with its unique set of characteristics, strengths, and weaknesses. For instance, some introverts might be creative and imaginative, preferring to express themselves through art, while others might be analytical and thoughtful, enjoying problem-solving activities. Extroverts also have their variances. Some might be natural leaders, thriving in roles where they can guide and inspire others, while others might excel in roles that require teamwork and collaboration.

The MBTI looks at how you prefer to interact with the world by examining four different aspects of your personality. These aspects include whether you're more introverted (I) or extroverted (E), use sensing (S) or intuition (N) more, favor thinking (T) or feeling (F), and judge (J) or perceive (P) things more. This results in a total of 16 potential personality types.

Below are the descriptions of the eight types each for introverts and extroverts.

Introverted Types:

1. ISTJ - The Inspector
   - Detail-oriented, practical, and organized.
   - Values loyalty, responsibility, and tradition.

2. ISFJ - The Protector
   - Kind, reliable, and conscientious.
   - Cares deeply for others and seeks harmony and cooperation.

3. INFJ - The Counselor

   - Idealistic, insightful, and compassionate.
   - Values deep, authentic relationships.

4. INTJ - The Mastermind

   - Innovative, strategic, and logical.
   - Values competence, knowledge, and structure.

5. ISTP - The Craftsman

   - Observant, practical, and efficient.
   - Values freedom and flexibility.

6. ISFP - The Composer

   - Sensitive, creative, and kind.
   - Values harmony, beauty, and personal expression.

7. INFP - The Healer

   - Idealistic, creative, and compassionate.
   - Values authenticity, growth, and potential.

8. INTP - The Architect

   - Analytical, imaginative, and innovative.
   - Values knowledge, competence, and problem-solving.

Extroverted Types:

1. ESTJ - The Supervisor
   - Organized, decisive, and practical.
   - Values order, structure, and efficiency.

2. ESFJ - The Provider
   - Caring, sociable, and supportive.
   - Values cooperation, harmony, and kindness.

3. ENFJ - The Teacher
   - Inspirational, empathetic, and reliable.
   - Values personal growth, cooperation, and harmony.

4. ENTJ - The Commander
   - Strategic, confident, and dynamic.
   - Values competence, innovation, and results.

5. ESTP - The Dynamo
   - Energetic, practical, and adaptable.
   - Values experience, flexibility, and problem-solving.

6. ESFP - The Performer
   - Enthusiastic, spontaneous, and energetic.
   - Values fun, excitement, and spontaneity.

7. ENFP - The Champion
   - Creative, enthusiastic, and warm.
   - Values creativity, growth, and freedom.

8. ENTP - The Visionary
   - Innovative, entrepreneurial, and visionary.
   - Values knowledge, competence, and possibilities.

These 16 personality types, each with its unique characteristics, provide insights into personal growth, career paths, and relationship dynamics. Recognizing your type and understanding its dynamics can help you navigate bumping dots in your personal and professional life.

Bumping Dots with Different Personality Types

The concept of Bumping Dots beautifully highlights the intricate world of human connections, demonstrating how diverse personalities can gracefully converge. When integrating the Myers-Briggs Type Indicator (MBTI) and its spectrum of 16 distinct personalities, this concept illuminates the various ways in which unique individuals can meaningfully interact. Let's explore how these various personality types might bump dots with one another:

- ***ISTJ (The Inspector) & ISFJ (The Protector):***
  Envision these types as dots that have a consistent and steady pace. They're like the dots that move in straight lines, preferring predictability. When they collide with extroverted dots, there can be a momentary pause as they realign and adjust their direction. Tradition, consistency, and practicality are values shared by both personality types. When bumping into other dots, they may find inconsistency and unpredictability challenging. However, they provide grounding and can act as stabilizing forces in their interactions.

- ***INFJ (The Counselor) & INTJ (The Mastermind):***
  These dots might be visualized as having a deep and layered trajectory, often seeming to move with purpose and depth. When they interact with surface-level dots, they might either inspire them to add layers or move past to find dots with similar depth. These intuitive types, often with a future-oriented vision, might run into challenges when bumping dots with personality types that focus heavily on the present or tangible facts. They, however, offer depth and foresight in discussions.

- ***ISTP (The Craftsman) & ISFP (The Composer):***
  These dots are the adaptive ones. They can quickly change direction upon collision, making them versatile in interactions. Their flexibility might, however, cause friction with dots that prefer set pathways. These are adaptable realists. Their bumping interactions could be smooth, as they generally "go with the flow." They might, however, face challenges with types that require extensive planning and structure`.

- ***INFP (The Healer) & INTP (The Architect):*** Imagine these dots as being vibrant, adding color wherever they go. When they bump into more neutral dots, they either add some of their hues to them or move along, seeking more vibrant interactions. These types seek authenticity. They may not want to connect if they perceive superficiality or when they feel their values are challenged. Their strength lies in their innovative ideas and depth of feeling.

- ***ESTP (The Dynamo) & ESFP (The Performer):***
  These are the lively, fast-moving dots on the canvas. They easily attract other dots but might find friction with slower-moving or overly cautious dots. Social and spontaneous, they often maneuver past these interactions with grace. Their challenges might arise

when they interact with personalities that require long-term planning or introspection, but they infuse energy and dynamism into interactions.

- ***ENFP (The Champion) & ENTP (The Visionary):***
These dots are the explorers, darting here and there with enthusiasm. They thrive when meeting other explorative dots but might find the straight liners (like ISTJs) a tad restrictive. As enthusiastic innovators, they're constantly seeking new possibilities. They may grow frustrated with personalities that are resistant to change or too tied to tradition. However, they're the sparks in brainstorming sessions.

- ***ESTJ (The Supervisor) & ESFJ (The Provider):***
Envision these as larger dots, often gathering smaller dots around them in structured patterns. They bring order but might clash with dots that resist their organized approach. They value structure and community. When bumping dots, they might find it hard when others challenge established norms or aren't team players. Yet, they are often the glue holding groups together.

- ***ENFJ (The Teacher) & ENTJ (The Commander):*** These charismatic dots tend to influence the direction of those they encounter. They often gather groups of dots, leading them towards a collective goal. However, dots that value autonomy might steer clear of their path. They are charismatic leaders with a vision. Frustration arises when they perceive a lack of initiative or decisiveness in others. They shine as motivators and strategic thinkers.

The Bumping Dots concept, when intertwined with the understanding of the MBTI personality types, facilitates more authentic interactions. It enables us to adapt and build meaningful connections across personalities we encounter. The potential for growth, learning, and mutual understanding is boundless, creating a world where each interaction is a step towards unity and shared human experience.

Tip: Although one's personality type may not be apparent or easily identifiable upon first contact, through the course of your engagement you may notice themes that align with the content shared that can help you bump dots more effectively. Connecting with someone different from you isn't about changing them or changing yourself; it's about understanding where they're coming from and finding common ground.

Embracing Adaptability in Interactions

In the world of Bumping Dots, we recognize that differences and potential conflicts can emerge. It's crucial to view these moments as opportunities to adjust our approach. Like dots that shift and change paths, individuals too can adapt their stance, ensuring more positive interactions.

Daniel Goleman's significant work in 1995 highlighted the essential role of emotional intelligence in our interactions. It's about recognizing, understanding, and managing our emotions, along with positively impacting others' emotions. With a honed emotional intelligence, maneuvering through diverse personalities becomes a more navigable and harmonious experience.

Strategies for Extroverts and Introverts to Effectively Bump Dots

Extroverts

For extroverts, Bumping Dots is an exciting landscape of possibilities. Enhance your impromptu interactions by considering these strategies:

- **Practice Patience:** Be mindful that not everyone may share your pace. Allow people the time they need to think and respond, nurturing a comfortable space for unexpected interactions.

- **Prioritize Listening:** Amidst the eagerness to share, take a moment to actively listen. Your attention can transform a casual interaction into a significant connection. Note: Many introverts value deeper conversations, so be mindful of cues that it is time to transition from small talk.

- **Welcome Feedback:** Encourage people to share how they feel about your interactions. Their insights can help you modify your approach, ensuring a positive experience for both parties in unexpected encounters.

- **Diversify Your Social Engagement:** Participate in various social activities and groups. It not only enriches your social life but also eases the pressure on any one specific relationship in your life, making encounters more relaxed and enjoyable for all.

- **Embrace Self-Reflection:** Dedicate time to introspect. Understanding yourself better enables you to adapt and improve your interactions, making every serendipitous interaction more fulfilling.

- **Respect Boundaries:** Understand and honor the boundaries others set. Recognize their need for space or quiet time as a form of self-care, not a rejection toward you or inadequacy on their part, ensuring every unexpected interaction is respectful and considerate.

Introverts

Navigating the world of spontaneous encounters can seem daunting for an introvert. However, here are some strategies that can help you embrace the unexpected and thrive in the world of Bumping Dots:

- **Anticipate Breaks:** When stepping out, mentally schedule in pauses. Even a moment of quiet can renew your energy and prepare you for unanticipated social interactions.

- **Be Open about Your Needs:** If a chance encounter turns into a prolonged conversation, it's okay to express your comfort level and boundaries. Your openness will foster understanding and make impromptu interactions more enjoyable.

- **Leverage Your Listening:** Use your natural listening skills in unexpected encounters. Listening attentively can alleviate the stress of leading the conversation. When interacting with extroverts, provide positive feedback and affirmations to encourage their expressiveness.

- **Have Topics Ready:** Keep a mental list of general topics or questions. Being prepared can ease anxiety during unexpected conversations, allowing you to engage more comfortably.

- **Prioritize Smaller Settings:** In any situation, consider seeking out one-on-one or smaller group interactions. These environments, even in unexpected scenarios, can feel more manageable and enjoyable.

- **Use Written Expressions:** If spontaneous face-to-face conversations feel overwhelming, follow up with a thoughtful email or message. This approach allows you to communicate thoughtfully and at your own pace after a chance encounter.

Whether introverted or extroverted, aligning with the Bumping Dots concept means embracing flexibility in our interactions. By finding common ground, we can use shared interests and goals as a foundation to build a connection. As we adjust our approach and honor each person's unique personality traits, we foster more understanding and respectful connections.

Moving past platitudes opens doors to meaningful connections. Deeper questions reveal the true stories of the dots we meet.

CHAPTER EIGHT

What Happens When You Dig Deeper?

Let's face it: we've all been caught in the endless loop of "Hi, how are you?" "Good, thanks!" These polite exchanges, while customary, seldom forge a path to meaningful connections. It's as if two dots are floating aimlessly in space, passively waiting to collide and create something significant.

Several years ago, I found myself at a friend's party, caught in a déjà vu of exchanges: "Hi, how have you been?" "Good, thanks, and you?" This pattern repeated with at least a dozen people. By the time I left, I couldn't recall a single meaningful conversation. It dawned on me—how many opportunities had slipped by? Any one of those encounters could have led to a delightful conversation about someone's latest adventure abroad or their journey learning a new instrument. Instead, I walked away with nothing but a collection of pleasantries.

This realization emphasizes the importance of heightened awareness in the cultivation of presence—being truly attentive and emotionally and mentally engaged, as well as asking the right questions. By attuning to your own emotions and those of others, you become sensitive to the subtleties that might otherwise remain unnoticed.

Being Present to Dig Deeper

Active participation in conversations is the essence of being present. It's about being fully engaged, not just passively listening, and it requires responding and contributing in a way that adds depth to the dialogue. Gratitude can illuminate our moments of interaction, infusing them with warmth and connecting us to the now in a profound way. This is because when you regularly take stock of the elements in your life that spark gratitude, you build a strong emotional and mental foundation, enhancing your ability to truly be present. Quality interactions naturally stem from such a presence, and encountering someone new offers a luminous opportunity to express gratitude by anchoring yourself in the current moment. A brief but concentrated conversation, where all participants are entirely engaged, can be more impactful and satisfying than hours of unfocused or shallow chatter. The depth of connection that can be achieved in these moments is priceless.

To sharpen your ability to stay present, immerse yourself in hobbies that captivate your full attention. Engage in activities that challenge and absorb you completely—be it creating an intricate painting, playing a video game, or tending to a garden. These activities require your focused engagement, helping you to refine the art of being present. In turn, the joy and tranquility they bring help you to realize the importance of going about your day with a centered and attentive spirit. As you approach each day, set your intentions with clarity and purpose to savor each moment fully.

This conscious commitment deepens your Bumping Dots experiences, transforming even the most mundane exchanges into opportunities for connection.

The Blueprint to Elevate Your Conversations

It's a disheartening feeling to converse with someone who seems a world away – their mind lost in a digital device or preoccupied with a different thought, resembling a dot meandering without purpose. To engage in the dance of Bumping Dots, it's crucial to be wholly present - not just physically but emotionally and mentally as well. The following is a simple way to elevate your conversation:

- <u>Seek Common Ground:</u> Think of this as the gravitational pull between two dots. Finding a mutual interest, whether it's a recent travel experience, a shared hobby, or even a favorite TV show, creates an instant bond and a pathway to deeper topics.

- <u>Share Something Personal:</u> Letting someone into your world by sharing a snippet from your life is like allowing your dot to glow, making it more visible and attractive. It doesn't have to be dramatic; it just needs to be genuine. Maybe it's a childhood memory of a fishing trip or the story of how you adopted your pet from a rescue shelter.

During a flight delay, I struck up a conversation with a woman beside me. We began with casual remarks about travel hassles. On a whim, I decided to share a humorous story about the time I missed my flight and had to stay an extra day in a city that I didn't want to be in. It led her to share her story of an impromptu hiking adventure in New Zealand. What started as complaints about a flight delay turned into a lively exchange of travel tales, all because we dared to share a bit of our own story.

Stoking Curiosity: The Catalyst of Connection

Like two dots hesitating before eventually bumping, our conversations need a catalyst, a spark, to delve deeper. Here's where curiosity and the art of questioning come into play. Curiosity transforms superficial small talk into profound interactions. It's not about prying into someone's life but expressing genuine interest in who they are. Thoughtful questions invite them to open up and reveal captivating depths you never knew were there. The key is that your curiosity must be authentic.

I saw this at a wedding when I asked an old friend, "What exciting things have you been up to lately?" Turns out he was an avid fisherman who competed in tournaments. We talked for hours about equipment, favorite fishing holes, and types of fish. It was a conversation I still cherish, all because I stoked my curiosity about his world.

Here are some curiosity-sparking questions to ask while bumping dots:

- What's the most fascinating thing you've learned recently?

- What books have you read lately?

- If you could visit anywhere in the world, where would you go?

- What challenges have you overcome that you feel proud of?

- What are you passionate about that most people don't know?

- What film scene last made you cry or laugh uncontrollably?

- What is a funny talent or special skill set that you have that most people are unaware of?

Lean in with eagerness to understand their experiences. This is when the magic happens, and the dots start converging in wondrous ways.

Why is Listening So Crucial?

Listening is the foundation of meaningful human interactions; its power lies in its ability to make you feel cared for and to allow the conversation to continue evolving. The five stages of listening include receiving (the act of hearing), understanding, evaluating, remembering, and responding. So, when bumping dots, you move beyond simply hearing another dot toward gaining an understanding of their needs and learning how to respond and progress in the bumping exchange.

How to Listen Actively:

- **Maintain Eye Contact:** This simple gesture reinforces your presence and attentiveness.

- **Nod and Offer Encouragement:** Simple things like "mm-hmm" or "I see" can go a long way.

- **Avoid Interrupting:** Let them finish their thoughts before sharing your perspective.

- **Clarify and Reflect:** If you need clarification, repeat what you heard. For example, "So, you're saying..." or "What do you mean by..."

- **Show Empathy:** Phrases like "That must have been tough" or "I can imagine how you felt" display understanding and compassion.

Next time your conversation drifts in the vastness of the mundane, remember the secret of Bumping Dots. By listening, being present, and being curious, you can move forward. Take in the wonder of a serendipitous moment as it unfolds around you.

Beyond Small Talk

During the writing of *Bumping Dots*, I drew on personal experiences to build the narrative. All of us have experienced those chance encounters that changed our lives. In 2006, a friend invited me to hear Joseph B. Washington II, the insightful author of *Let Average Go*, speak at a network marketing event.

Joseph stood in front of the crowd and spoke about rising above mediocrity, pushing boundaries, and inspiring change. Drawn to his message, I felt compelled to introduce myself. Our initial conversation was memorable. Joseph's magnetic personality, combined with his honest kindness, made it feel like we'd known each other for years.

From that day, our interactions transformed from being mere acquaintances to trusted confidants. We discussed our writings, our philosophies, and our hopes for the future. Our professional interests in writing and personal development provided a foundation, but it was our shared perspectives and values that truly deepened our connection.

Joseph and I began mentoring each other in various aspects of our lives. Our relationship was reciprocal, characterized by mutual admiration, respect, and a shared thirst for knowledge and growth. The power of time is remarkable in its ability to either weaken or strengthen connections. In our case, our friendship only grew stronger with each passing year.

Strategies to Digging Deeper with Your Dots

Effective communication is more than just exchanging words; it's about conveying emotions, intentions, and understanding. Here's a deeper look into some strategies that have helped strengthen the bond that Joseph and I have:

- **Be an Active Listener:** Genuine listening is about more than just hearing words; it's about grasping the emotions and ideas behind them. When Joseph discusses a new concept or recounts a personal anecdote, active listening ensures that I fully understand not just the content but also the underlying sentiments. Such attentive listening fosters trust, demonstrating an investment in the other person's experiences and feelings.

- **Build Trust:** Our relationship's strength lies in being vulnerable and authentic, which has built mutual trust. Over time, as our relationship has flourished, we've found more areas of our lives we're comfortable discussing. As trust deepens, it paves the way for more personal and heartfelt conversations.

- **Embrace Dialogue, Not Monologue:** Both parties should contribute, building on each other's insights. Through interactive dialogue, Joseph and I often explore new perspectives, which pushes both of us to rethink our perceptions.

- **Seek and Provide Feedback:** It's important to create a space for constructive feedback. This not only involves asking for areas of improvement but also sharing insights about the other's approach. Joseph and I have regular "health checks" in the form of reflective conversations to ensure our relationship remains dynamic, meeting each other's evolving needs.

- **Acknowledge and Validate:** Small gestures, such as nodding or affirming with words, can significantly enhance a conversation. Whenever Joseph and I share experiences, acknowledging each other validates the importance of our feelings and experiences, further enhancing our connection.

The connection I've fostered with Joseph B. Washington epitomizes digging deeper. While deliberate endeavors anchored our relationship, the spontaneous, unscripted moments often infused the most richness and depth into our connection. Allowing space for organic growth turned out to be equally crucial as any planned strategy. In a way, our moments of bumping dots served as checkpoints, reinforcing the strength and value of our friendship.

While we can plan and strategize, some of the most profound moments occur when we least expect them. It is vital that you cherish those serendipitous moments and unexpected encounters, as they may just be the threads that bind you for life. In Bumping Dots, it's not just the dots that count, but also how they connect.

The Ripple Effect

Our connection ultimately has led to us expanding our professional and personal dot connections. For instance, Joseph introduced me to a consultant who assisted me in promoting *Bumping Dots*. In turn, my insights from higher education enabled him to connect with administrators, which led to speaking opportunities for his book. Moreover, during a recent trip where I supported Joseph at a speaking engagement, we both had the chance to meet and connect with other education professionals. It's remarkable to consider that this all began with a friend inviting me to a networking event where I met Joseph.

Consider the unseen ripple effect as the silent impact that each interaction carries with it. It's the phone call with a friend, who then feels uplifted and goes on to help a colleague with a project. It's the smile shared with a stranger who then carries that positivity into their home, brightening the day of their family members. The echoes of our interactions have the power to travel through time and space, touching various lives in unexpected ways. Every shared laugh, every word of encouragement, and every gesture of kindness contributes to a cascade of effects, shaping the world one interaction at a time.

The long-term impacts of every dot collision do not unfold instantaneously. The seeds planted while bumping dots may take days, months, or even years to bloom. A chance encounter today might influence a significant life decision in the future. A seemingly inconsequential chat could sow the seeds for a new career, passion, or partnership down the line. An exchange of ideas today could lay the foundation for innovation and collaboration in the years to come. Recognizing these possibilities underscores the significance of each interaction, casting it in the light of potentiality and future impact.

Understanding the ripple effect of bumping dots calls us to tread the paths of interaction with heightened mindfulness and intentionality. It pushes us to peer beyond the surface of casual conversations and recognize the latent potential cradled within our interactions. It encourages the acknowledgment of the profound power embedded in our words, gestures, and presence. This awareness transforms each encounter and each dialogue into a meaningful exchange, imbued with respect, empathy, and openness.

As you reach the end of this book, think of it as the first step on a new journey. Every day brings a chance to bump dots with someone new.

CHAPTER NINE
Final Thoughts: Keep Bumping

My Fearless Dot, if this was a novel, you're now turning to its climactic chapter. It's difficult to believe we're already at this point, isn't it? From those initial tentative steps to this confident stride you now possess, it's been transformative.

This chapter is not simply words on paper. Imagine it as a jubilant gathering, where every connection you've made, every dot you've bumped into, comes together in celebration. Hear the pop of the confetti cannons, see the sundry colors dancing around you, and feel the warmth of accomplishment. The virtual high-five we're sharing, not just for the destination but also for the multifarious paths you've encountered, the hurdles you've overcome, and the resilience you've showcased.

So, let's not merely skim through this chapter. Instead, let's dive in, immersing ourselves in a reflective pool of memories, learnings, and the sheer joy of "connecting the dots." While this chapter might mark the culmination of this book, it's just the beginning of your lifelong adventure in Bumping Dots.

Let's savor it, rejoice in it, and bask in all we've achieved. Ready to dive in?

Taking Stock of the Connections Made

Taking a moment to reflect on the connections made and the lessons learned can be a knowledgeable and enriching experience. Think back to the beginning of this adventure when you, that eager-to-connect dot, picked up this book driven by curiosity. Yes, that was you, and it's remarkable to see how far you've come.

Starting with our Bumping Dots mindset, our lives begin to resemble intricate webs, with each bump representing a unique experience or encounter. Perhaps you bumped into a dot while exploring a new hobby, which unexpectedly led you to bump into a dot in your community, paving the way for you to discover a career that resonates further with your passions, where other dots awaited you. Life often unfolds in ways we could not have imagined.

Take pride in how far you've come, celebrate the connections you've formed, and cherish the lessons you've learned. Embrace the unpredictable beauty of life's interconnected dots, for they continue to guide you on your path of discovery and growth.

How to Make Bumping Dots a Lifestyle

You know how some people have incorporated practices like meditation into their daily lives, and it's not just an activity but also a way of existing? Bumping Dots can be visualized similarly. It's more than a method—it's a lifestyle, a mindset. It stretches your mind, enriching your perspective and widening your circle of connections.

Imagine living every day, actively searching for patterns, links, and connections in your daily interactions and experiences. It's nurturing for the soul, creating an ecosystem where you're continually learning and growing. Plus, by recognizing and acting on these connections, you're not only enriching your own life but also potentially adding value to the lives of those around you.

Once again, consider these additions to your Bumping Dots toolkit—a collection of exercises designed to enhance your journey:

- **Morning Dot Meditation:** As you start your day, envision the people you might serendipitously encounter. By dedicating a few minutes each morning to visualize the connections you hope to make, you're essentially programming your mind to be alert and receptive. This isn't just about meeting new people or learning new things; it's about an active engagement with the world. By doing so, even your routine tasks can become exciting opportunities.

- **Monthly Dot Check-in:** Taking monthly checks isn't just about tallying numbers; it's also about understanding the depth and breadth of connections made. Perhaps you reached out to an old friend, or maybe you discovered a new hobby. By setting aside time each month, you can appreciate the richness these connections bring to your life. It's also an excellent opportunity to set goals for the next month. Which dots do you want to explore further? Which dots did you miss?

- **Dot-Aid Kit:** Let's face it, we've all been in situations where we've felt out of depth or faced awkward silences. This is where your "Dot-Aid Kit" comes in. A mental toolkit of open-ended questions or conversation starters can be a lifesaver. They're your bridge to potential connections. Maybe you're waiting in line for a service, or you're at a social event where you don't know anyone. By initiating a conversation, you're opening the door to a world of new dots. Who knows, the person you talk to in the grocery line could introduce you to your next favorite book, hobby, or even a future collaboration!

- **Serendipity Gatherings:** Attend events without a particular goal. Instead of networking in the traditional sense, remain open to the chance of bumping into someone new and allowing the conversation to unfold organically.

- **Chat Adventures:** Change your daily routine by, for example, visiting a different restaurant or taking a different route via walking or public transportation. Strike up spontaneous conversations, discovering the stories and backgrounds of those you meet.

- **Local Dot Exploration:** Walk around your neighborhood or town with open eyes and ears, ready to engage in unexpected conversations. It's amazing how many potential dots live or work just around the corner!

- **Dot Exchange:** Organize or participate in a "Meet Someone New" day at work, church, or in your community, where the goal is purely to connect with someone you haven't interacted with before.

- **Deep Dive with New Dots:** Whenever you meet a new dot, invest some time in getting to know them beyond surface-level interactions. Unearth the mutual interests or experiences that might've otherwise gone unnoticed.

- **Cultural Dot Exploration:** Attend cultural events or festivals in your city. It's a beautiful way to bump into dots from diverse backgrounds, broadening your horizon and understanding of the world through personal stories.

Embracing Bumping Dots as a lifestyle is about cultivating an ever-curious mindset, one that's always on the lookout for patterns, learnings, and new experiences. So, are you ready to bump into some dots today?

Leaving the Door Open for All the Dots Yet to Come

Okay, if you lock the door and throw away the key, you're also saying goodbye to the wonderful world of dots awaiting you. And that's no way to live! To keep that door wide open, adopt a sense of childlike wonder for the world around you. Be open to new experiences, unexplored avenues, and yes, more dots. Whether it's traveling internationally, taking an online course, or attending a cooking class—each experience has a world of dots waiting to be bumped into. These dots may introduce you to new passions, connections, or insights you never imagined.

So, let's keep bumping dots. Here's to many more dots, connections, and the beautiful web they weave. Cheers to the adventures yet to come, the lessons to be learned, and the people to meet along the way. May your life be filled with wonders and discoveries as you continue to bump into the dots that shape your unique path.

As you close this book, you're not bidding farewell to the concept; rather you're stepping into a world swarming with dots, each with its own potential to enrich, enlighten, and entertain. In a way, finishing this book is itself a dot connection. And who knows, perhaps we'll bump into each other someday in the intricate maze of dots that is life.

LET'S KEEP THE CONVERSATION GOING!
Bump Dots With Me on Social Media

- Instagram & Twitter (X): @drherbthomas
- TikTok: @bumpingdots
- Facebook: Herb Thomas
- LinkedIn: linkedin.com/in/drherbthomas06

Contact for Other Products or Speaking Engagements

Website: http://www.drherbthomas.com
Email: contact@respublishingandbranding.com

Bumping Dots with the Docs PODCAST

Tune in to our podcast, where I team up with my daughter, Dr. Ashley C. Thomas, for enriching conversations. Find us on YouTube and Apple Podcasts.

DR. HERB THOMAS

Dr. Herb Thomas, Jr. stands at the forefront of leadership training, bringing together his passion for education and a mission to empower others to find their purpose. With an educational foundation from Alabama State University and a Ph.D. from the University of Missouri-Columbia, Herb has made significant strides in both academic and ministry settings through his visionary leadership. With over 25 years in higher education administration and mentoring, he remains dedicated to nurturing students, guiding them to excel as leaders in their professional fields, communities, and personal lives.

In addition to his professional endeavors, Herb is deeply committed to personal growth and continuous learning. An explorer at heart, Herb's global adventures have added diversity to his perspective, and his love for travel is matched only by his voracious appetite for knowledge. Engaging in a wide array of reading materials, he consistently incorporates fresh insights, current affairs, and ideas into his teachings. This lifelong pursuit of knowledge not only enriches Herb's own life but also enhances his ability to inspire and empower the upcoming generation of leaders. His enthusiasm for sports, especially softball, further highlights his commitment to teamwork, healthy competition, and supportive relationships.

At the heart of Herb's life is his family, with whom he shares a profound dedication to education, faith, and service. Together with his wife, Dr. Christine C. Thomas, and their daughters, Dr. Ashley and Duchess Kimberly, they produce *LEGACY eMagazine* (*https://issuu.com/legacyemagazine*). This monthly publication highlights the achievements and stories of entrepreneurs and leaders from around the globe, amplifying the Thomas family's impact on fostering a legacy of inspiration and influence. Dr. Herb Thomas, Jr.'s combination of professional achievements, personal ethos, and natural motivational talent embodies authentic leadership and the ability to effect genuine change.

Made in the USA
Columbia, SC
01 May 2024

34849340R00074